Growing Readers

New Hanover County Public Library

Purchased with
New Hanover County Partnership for Children
and Smart Start Funds

Let's Read About Our Bodies

Hands

by Cynthia Klingel and Robert B. Noyed
photographs by Gregg Andersen

*Amoroso is preferred name

Reading consultant: Cecilia Minden-Cupp, Ph.D.,
Adjunct Professor, College of Continuing and Professional Studies, University of Virginia

Weekly Reader.
EARLY LEARNING LIBRARY

For a free color catalog describing Weekly Reader® Early Learning Library's list of high-quality books, call 1-800-542-2595 or fax your request to (414) 332-3567.

Library of Congress Cataloging-in-Publication Data

Klingel, Cynthia.
  Hands / by Cynthia Klingel and Robert B. Noyed.
    p. cm. — (Let's read about our bodies)
  Includes bibliographical references and index.
  Summary: An introduction to hands, what they are used for, and how to take care of them.
  ISBN 0-8368-3066-0 (lib. bdg.)
  ISBN 0-8368-3155-1 (softcover)
  1. Hand—Juvenile literature. [1. Hand.] I. Noyed, Robert B. II. Title.
  QM548.K554   2002
  611'.97—dc21   2001055055

This edition first published in 2002 by
Weekly Reader® Early Learning Library
330 West Olive Street, Suite 100
Milwaukee, WI 53212 USA

An Editorial Directions book
Editors: E. Russell Primm and Emily Dolbear
Art direction, design, and page production: The Design Lab
Photographer: Gregg Andersen
Weekly Reader® Early Learning Library art direction: Tammy Gruenewald
Weekly Reader® Early Learning Library production: Susan Ashley

Printed in the United States of America

1 2 3 4 5 6 7 8 9 06 05 04 03 02

Note to Educators and Parents

As a Reading Specialist I know that books for young children should engage their interest, impart useful information, and motivate them to want to learn more.

Let's Read About Our Bodies is a new series of books designed to help children understand the value of good health and taking care of their bodies.

A young child's active mind is engaged by the carefully chosen subjects. The imaginative text works to build young vocabularies. The short, repetitive sentences help children stay focused as they develop their own relationship with reading. The bright, colorful photographs of children enjoying good health habits complement the text with their simplicity and both entertain and encourage young children to want to learn — and read — more.

These books are designed to be used by adults as "read-to" books to share with children to encourage early literacy in the home, school, and library. They are also suitable for more advanced young readers to enjoy on their own.

— Cecilia Minden-Cupp, Ph.D.,
Adjunct Professor, College of Continuing and
Professional Studies, University of Virginia

These are my hands.

I have two hands.

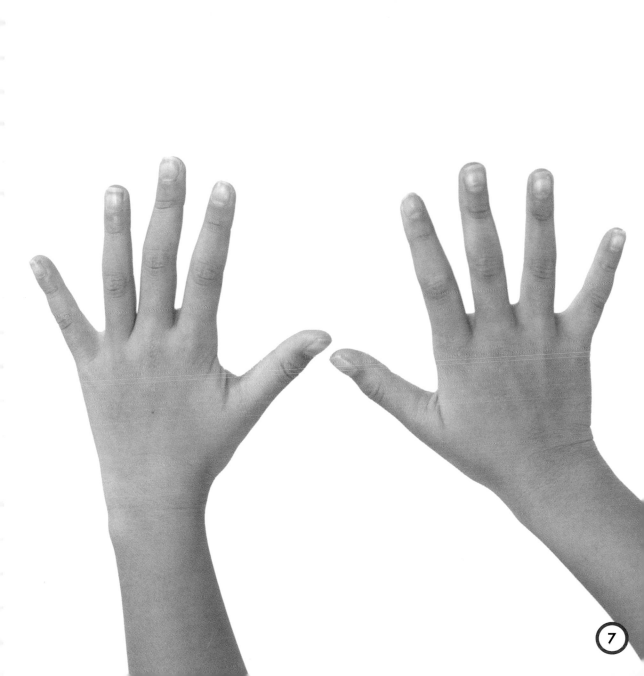

I have ten fingers. Five fingers are on each hand.

I have ten fingernails. I keep them short and clean.

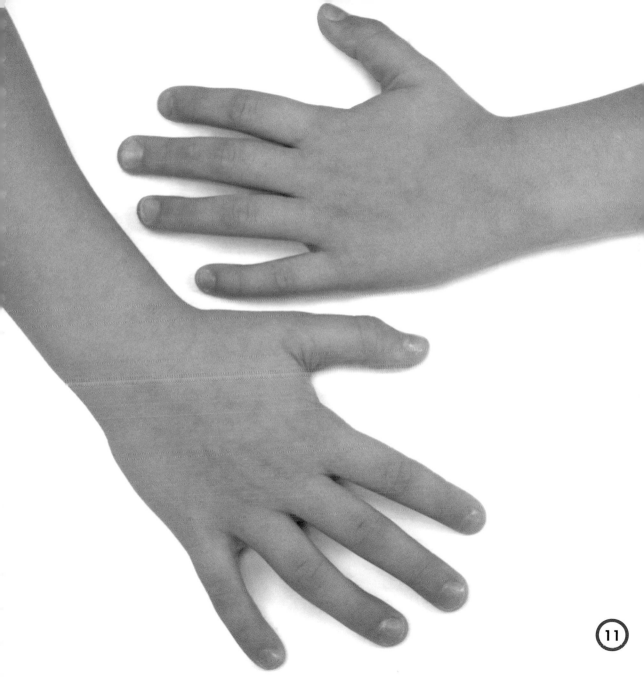

11

I can pick up my
toys with my hands.

I can clap with
my hands.

I keep my hands warm. I wear mittens when it is cold.

I keep my hands clean. I wash with soap and water.

I can even stand
on my hands!
Can you?

Glossary

clap—to strike your hands together for enjoyment

fingernails—a thin, hard layer of material growing at the end of each finger

mittens—warm coverings for the hands

For More Information

Fiction Books

Ehlert, Lois. *Hands*. San Diego: Harcourt Brace, 1997.

Ross, Tony. *Wash Your Hands*. Brooklyn, N.Y.: Kane/Miller, 2000.

Ryder, Joanne. *My Father's Hands*. New York: William Morrow, 1994.

Nonfiction Books

Agassi, Martine. *Hands Are Not for Hitting*. Minneapolis: Free Spirit Press, 2000

Kroll, Virginia. *Hands!* Honesdale, Penn.: Boyds Mills Press, 1997.

Web Sites
Why Do I Need to Wash My Hands?
kidshealth.org/kid/talk/qa/wash_hands.html
For information about why you should wash your hands

Index

caring for, 10, 16, 18
clapping, 14
cleaning, 10, 18
fingernails, 10
fingers, 8

handstands, 20
keeping warm, 16
mittens, 16
washing, 18

About the Authors

Cynthia Klingel has worked as a high school English teacher and an elementary school teacher. She is currently the curriculum director for a Minnesota school district. Cynthia Klingel lives with her family in Mankato, Minnesota.

Robert B. Noyed started his career as a newspaper reporter. Since then, he has worked in school communications and public relations at the state and national level. Robert B. Noyed lives with his family in Brooklyn Center, Minnesota.